Dr.
Seuss

Other titles in the Inventors and Creators series include:

Benjamin Franklin
Henry Ford
Jim Henson
Jonas Salk
Thomas Edison

Dr.
Seuss

P.M. Boekhoff and
Stuart A. Kallen

KIDHAVEN PRESS

THOMSON

———————✦———————™

GALE

Detroit • New York • San Diego • San Francisco
Boston • New Haven, Conn. • Waterville, Maine
London • Munich

On cover: Dr. Seuss drawing at his desk.

Library of Congress Cataloging-in-Publication Data

Boekhoff, P.M. (Patti Marlene), 1957–
   Dr. Seuss / by P.M. Boekhoff and Stuart A. Kallen.
      p. cm.
Summary: Discusses the childhood, education, influences, marriage, and writing career of the author known as Dr. Seuss.
   ISBN 0-7377-0997-9 (hardback : alk. paper)
   1. Seuss, Dr.—Juvenile literature. 2. Authors, American—20th century—Biography—Juvenile literature. 3. Illustrators—United States—Biography—Juvenile literature. 4. Children's literature—Authorship—Juvenile literature. [1. Seuss, Dr. 2. Authors, American. 3. Illustrators.] I. Title: Doctor Seuss. II. Kallen, Stuart A., 1995– . III. Title
   PS3513 E.2 Z59 2002
   813' .52—dc21

2001004397

Copyright 2002 by KidHaven Press,
an imprint of The Gale Group
10911 Technology Place, San Diego, CA 92127

Printed in the U.S.A.

Contents

A Champion Among Children

Dr. Seuss, whose real name was Theodor Seuss Geisel, was an American author, artist, and **publisher** who wrote more than forty books for children. His stories such as *How the Grinch Stole Christmas, The Cat in the Hat,* and *Green Eggs and Ham* have sold millions of copies and have been made into movies, cartoons, and television specials.

The stories of Dr. Seuss are loved by children around the world, and they were written by an author who claims he never grew up himself because he never lost his joy for living. Even when his stories were rejected by dozens of publishers in the early days, he remained hopeful. And Dr. Seuss always kept his sense of humor because he believed that humor helps people cope with serious questions and problems in their lives. In *The Secret Art of Dr. Seuss* by Theodor Seuss Geisel, his friend Maurice Sendak said, "Dr. Seuss was serious about not being 'serious.'"[1]

Dr. Seuss lived life to the fullest. He loved wacky adventures, tall tales, and pleasures of the imagination. He

Dr. Seuss speaks with some of his young fans in 1957.

is a champion among children, and among adults as well, and millions believe that his stories have helped make the world a better place.

Chapter One

Theodor Seuss Geisel

Theodor Seuss Geisel was born on March 2, 1904 in Springfield, Massachusetts. When he was a young boy, he was known simply as Ted. Ted lived with his sister Marnie, his father Theodor R. Geisel, and his mother Henrietta Seuss Geisel, known as Nettie. Ted's father and grandfather worked together at the family brewery.

Ted's mother was a baker who often chanted the names of the pies she was making at the bakery in a soft lively rhythm to the children as they fell asleep at night. She also read many poetic tales to Marnie and Ted, and rewarded them with books when they were good. Ted quickly learned to read the books that his mother gave him.

Before long, Ted began chanting in a rhythm like his mother. His stories were outlandish tales about people he had seen on the street, the floats in the local parade, or even his grandfather's horse-drawn beer wagons rolling through town.

Ted had several books that inspired him to draw and write. One of those was *The Brownies: Their Book*, which contained pictures of fairies, goblins, and sprites who performed amusing pranks and good deeds. Another was *The Hole Book* by Peter Newell, which inspired Ted to begin writing his own stories at the age of six.

Amazing Animals

Ted did not have to look far for creative ideas. His house was near the Springfield Zoo, and when he was in his room, he could hear the chattering, cawing, and bellowing of the animals. Surrounded with books and doodled pictures, he made up marvelous stories about what he thought the animals were saying and doing.

Ted's father volunteered at the zoo, and he often took his son to see the lions, hippos, elephants, giraffes, bears, and other animals. Ted looked carefully at everything he

Dr. Seuss holds a sculpture of one of the many animals he thought up while a boy.

saw, sketching parts of different animals stuck together into one amazing creature that might have the trunk of an elephant, the long ears of a donkey, the bushy mane of a lion, and the wings of a bird.

When not making drawings, Ted amused his friends with silly stories. He seemed to remember everything, always stretching the truth to make people laugh. And he could wiggle his ears better than anybody in the neighborhood. He was also a joyful prankster, playing practical jokes on people. But everything changed when he was eleven years old.

The Outsider

In 1915, 1,195 people, (including 128 Americans) died on the *Lusitania*, a British ship torpedoed by a German submarine during World War I. Although the United States was not yet involved in the conflict, this act of war turned many Americans against people of German heritage, like the Geisels.

As German Americans, Ted's family spoke both German and English at home. Ted also read books written in German that he checked out of the library. After the *Lusitania* incident, German Americans were treated by some as enemies of the United States. German books disappeared from the libraries, and some were burned at anti-German rallies.

While Ted was walking to and from school, other children insulted and threw rocks at him. He later said that he was "chased home from school, being clobbered . . . with brickbats . . . [because he] was a kid with a German father."[2] But Ted kept a cheery face, unwilling to show his pain to the world.

High School Days

By the time the war ended in 1918, Ted was a sophomore in high school. The end of the fighting brought victory parades and new hopes that the clouds of suspicion and **prejudice** would lift from his family. But some Americans continued to discriminate against those of German heritage.

A 1915 newspaper article tells the grim story of the sinking of the *Lusitania*.

THE NEW YORK HERALD.

PART II.   NEW YORK, SATURDAY, MAY 8, 1915.—TWENTY-TWO PAGES   PRICE THREE CENTS.

THE LUSITANIA IS SUNK;
1,000 PROBABLY ARE LOST

GERMANS TORPEDO THE GIANT STEAMSHIP AND SHE FOUNDERS EIGHT MILES FROM IRISH COAST

RESCUE VESSELS SPEED TO THE SCENE TO PICK UP SURVIVORS; ONLY 500 ARE ACCOUNTED FOR

George A. Kessler One of Those Saved, Cable Message to Cunard Office Says

1,000 LIVES LOST, LAST ESTIMATE

Ted used his sense of humor to help him cope, drawing cartoons and writing poems for the weekly school newspaper, *The Revolver.* He reported on issues and wrote satire, using humor to make fun of mean-spirited or foolish behavior. Soon, he was writing so many pieces that he started signing some of them as T. S. LeSieg (Geisel spelled backward). And while he was still in high school, Ted vowed to make a living at something he loved to do—writing and drawing.

Jacko

In September 1921, Ted took a train to Dartmouth College, a private school in Hanover, New Hampshire. He planned to major in English. He was surprised to find that none of the clubs called **fraternities** asked him to join during **Pledge Week** when new members are recruited. Once again, prejudice made Ted an outsider. At that time many people discriminated against Jews, and they mistakenly thought Ted was Jewish because of his dark wavy hair and facial features.

Ted vowed to get a job on the school humor magazine *Jack-O-Lantern* or *Jacko,* to poke fun at the type of ignorance and prejudice that had excluded him from the fraternities. He told Judith and Neil Morgan, authors of *Dr. Seuss & Mrs. Geisel: A Biography:* "I think my interest in editing the Dartmouth humor magazine began . . . that Pledge Week."[3]

Ted spent most of his time writing for *Jacko,* and in his junior year was put in charge of running the paper. But in his senior year he got into trouble for drinking

Ted Geisel wrote for the school humor magazine while attending Dartmouth College (pictured).

and was forbidden to write for *Jacko*. He got around the rules by publishing his cartoons under other names, including Seuss and Thomas Mott Osborne—the Warden of Sing Sing Prison.

Love at First Sight

Since Ted wanted to become an English teacher after graduation, he decided to go to Oxford, a college in England, to seek an advanced degree. This degree would allow Ted to become a professor of literature—a teacher of creative writing—at a university or college.

One day, while he was doodling and daydreaming in class, a pretty American girl named Helen saw his drawings, and she said: "You're crazy to [want to] be a professor. . . . What you really want to do is draw. . . . That's a very fine flying cow!"[4] It was love at first sight, and Ted and Helen began to spend every spare minute together.

The couple traveled throughout Europe and later returned to America. Helen moved to New York City and Ted dropped out of Oxford, moving back to his parents' home. To raise enough money to be able to join Helen, Ted sent out cartoons to every newspaper and magazine he could think of in New York. Finally John Rose, an artist who had worked with him on *Jacko*, helped him to land a job at *Judge*, a political humor magazine. Ted mar-

Students change classes at Oxford University, England, where Ted Geisel attended graduate school.

A cover of the *Judge*, a political humor magazine where Ted Geisel worked after leaving Oxford.

ried Helen, and they moved into an apartment in New York City. He drew political cartoons of talking elephants and turtles stacked up to the sky, signing them "Dr. Seuss." It was the beginning of a promising career.

Chapter Two

Dr. Seuss

In 1927, married to his college sweetheart Helen, Ted Geisel was working as a cartoonist in New York City and signing his work "Dr. Seuss." After about four months at *Judge*, he drew a cartoon that would change his life. It was a picture of a knight lying on a bed in his castle with a dragon nuzzling up to him. The caption said, "Darn it all, another dragon. And just after I'd sprayed the whole castle with Flit."[5] Flit was a well-known **insecticide**.

The wife of the man in charge of advertising for Flit saw the cartoon in *Judge* and persuaded her husband to hire the talented artist to draw the company's ads. For the next seventeen years, Dr. Seuss made advertising history with his wildly successful cartoon ads. He drew all kinds of zany creatures and the caption on each cartoon said, "Quick, Henry! The Flit!"[6]

With income from the ads, Dr. Seuss and Helen were able to travel all over the world. By the time they had been married nine years, they had visited thirty countries in Europe, Latin America, and the Middle East.

In 1936 they were in Europe, where they heard anxious rumors that German dictator Adolf Hitler was about to plunge the continent into a horrible new war. The Geisels saw danger around every corner as their little tour bus climbed the steep Swiss mountain roads. Dr. Seuss sketched horned creatures dangling dangerously

One of the many cartoons drawn by Dr. Seuss that criticized Adolf Hitler.

from ledges in response to the dangerous political storms that were brewing.

A Story That No One Can Beat

The Geisels sailed back to New York over stormy seas that made the ship shake and shudder. Dr. Seuss became restless, wandering from lounge to lounge aboard the ship. Finally, according to the Morgans, he wrote a rambling story on the ship's stationery:

> A stupid horse and wagon . . . Horse and chariot . . . Chariot pulled by flying cat . . . Flying cat pulling Viking ship . . . Viking ship sailing up a volcano . . . Volcano blowing hearts, diamonds, and clubs . . . I saw a giant eight miles tall . . . Who took the cards, 52 in all . . . And played a game of solitaire.[7]

Listening to the rhythm of the ship's engines to keep his mind off the storms, Dr. Seuss began to recite verses. After a while, he started to recite "And that is a story that no one can beat, and to think that I saw it on Mulberry Street."[8]

When he got home, the rhythm stayed in his head. He said it was driving him crazy, and Helen thought it would help if he made a story from the words he put together on the ship, so he worked on verses for those quirky words, then drew pictures to go with them. He called the book *A Story That No One Can Beat*.

In 1937 Dr. Seuss sent his **manuscript** to twenty-seven different publishers. Everyone rejected the story

Dr. Seuss developed his rhythmic writing style while traveling aboard the MS *Kungsholm* (pictured).

because they thought it was too unusual and different from other children's books on the market. Dr. Seuss tells what happened next:

> I bumped into Mike McClintock [a friend from Dartmouth] coming down Madison Avenue. He said, "What's that under your arm?" I said, "That's a book no one will publish. I'm lugging it home to burn." Then I asked Mike, "What are *you* doing?" He said, "This morning I was appointed **juvenile editor** of Vanguard Press, and we happen to be standing in front of my office; would you like to come inside?"[9]

The president of Vanguard Press decided to publish the book if Dr. Seuss would give it a snappier title. Dr. Seuss decided to call it *And to Think That I Saw It on Mulberry Street*. He named the main character in the book Marco after Mike's son, to thank his old friend. Mulberry Street was the name of a real street in Springfield.

Hatching Horton

That chance meeting on the street with his old friend was one of the reasons Dr. Seuss always believed in good fortune, saying:

> Sometimes you have luck when you are doodling.
> I did one day when I was drawing some trees.
> Then I began drawing elephants. I had a window
> that was open, and the wind blew the elephant on

Springfield, Massachusetts (pictured), shows up in the Dr. Seuss book, *And to Think That I Saw It on Mulberry Street*.

top of a tree. I looked at it and said, "What do you suppose that elephant is doing there?" The answer was: "He is hatching an egg." Then all I had to do was write a book about it. I have left that window open ever since, but it's never happened again.[10]

Despite his good luck, Dr. Seuss struggled while writing his new book, unable to settle on a name for the elephant. First he chose Osmer, then Bosco, then Humphrey, and finally Horton, named after a Dartmouth classmate.

But Horton was put on hold when Hitler's troops moved into France. Instead Dr. Seuss turned his talents to drawing angry political cartoons about Adolf Hitler. Meanwhile, Horton was stuck in the tree and Dr. Seuss did not know how to get him down. It was Helen who finally wrote the words that hatched the elephant-bird, giving *Horton Hatches the Egg* a happy ending.

By this time, Dr. Seuss had a new publisher, Bennett Cerf of Random House, who loved the book so much he gave the Geisels more money than he had originally promised. The Geisels used the money to take a train from New York to La Jolla, California, where they began spending their summers.

Design for Death

Everyone, young and old, loved Horton. But Dr. Seuss was still haunted by Hitler and other foreign dictators. Dr. Seuss began to publish political cartoons about evil world leaders in a New York newspaper called *PM*, saying: "*PM* was against people who pushed other people around. I liked that."[11]

In 1941 the Japanese military bombed Pearl Harbor in Hawaii. The United States responded by declaring war on Japan, Germany, and Italy, whose dictators were allies in World War II.

Like many Americans, Dr. Seuss joined the military so that he could do more for the war effort. The author turned his talents to writing animated educational films for famed director Frank Capra's Army Signal Corps unit in Hollywood. Dr. Seuss and Capra shared a vision of hope for democracy, and they both liked to tell stories about the weak winning over the strong.

Dr. Seuss toured Europe with his educational film *Your Job in Germany*, showing it to the army generals

Director Frank Capra instructs visiting military staff on making a film.

there. Though the war was raging, Dr. Seuss wore his pistol upside down, since he never learned to shoot properly. The war ended in 1945 when Germany and Japan surrendered, as Italy had done in 1943.

Dr. Seuss returned to Hollywood, where he was offered many jobs in the film business, but he wanted to work with Helen on a history film that showed his sympathy for the Japanese people, whom he believed were victims of bad leaders. Their film, *Design for Death,* won an academy award for best documentary feature of 1947.

Chapter Three

A Few Choice Words

In the summer of 1947 the Geisels were enjoying a summer by the sea. Dr. Seuss stood on the terrace of a lovely villa in his pajamas, basking in the warm climate and the bright sunlit colors. Watercolor illustrations of fantasy fish were strewn around on the antique furniture.

The pictures were for the new Seuss book *McElligot's Pool*, a story in which Marco of *Mulberry Street* returns to tell a tale of how one small polluted pond might be connected to all the water on earth through an underground brook. When it was published, *McElligot's Pool* won Dr. Seuss his first Caldecott Medal, a prestigious award presented every year by the American Library Association to the artist of the best American picture book for children.

Success inspired Dr. Seuss to work long hours inventing new drawings and ideas. In addition he also accepted advertising commissions, even though too much work made his eyes hurt and he often had to visit the doctor. But the author's talents were paying well, and Dr. Seuss was able to buy a beautiful house

Dr. Seuss relaxes with his dog by his pool in La Jolla, California, in 1957.

on a hill in La Jolla that looked like a pink castle from a fairy tale. There, he worked in his new studio seven days a week.

In 1950 Dr. Seuss wrote *If I Ran the Zoo*, and he dedicated the book to his mother, Nettie, who had been writing a zoo book when he came home from college in 1927. It was Nettie's wordplay that had inspired him as a very young child, and his new book contained words and creatures that were stranger and more whimsical than ever.

No Matter How Small

It seemed that the more success Dr. Seuss achieved, the harder he worked. Helen often found him in his studio

A young girl delights in hearing, *If I Ran the Zoo.*

late at night hunched over drawings, and he rarely took a day off. In 1953, he was working on two projects at the same time—a full-length musical film called *The 5,000 Fingers of Dr. T* and the book *Scrambled Eggs Super!*

The 5,000 Fingers of Dr. T, about an evil piano teacher, was difficult to make however, and received some bad reviews. Dr. Seuss's script had been fought over and rewritten by so many people, that its lighthearted humor had lost much of its magic. Dr. Seuss said *Dr. T* caused "the greatest mass upchuck in the history of Hollywood,"[12] and the film project was "the worst experience of [my] life."[13]

To escape the bad film reviews, the Geisels traveled to Japan, where they visited Japanese schoolchildren.

Upon returning to La Jolla, Dr. Seuss wrote *Horton Hears a Who*, a book for the Japanese children he had met. The story is dedicated to the idea that every voice is important, no matter how small a person is.

The Geisels continued to juggle many responsibilities in their work and community. Suddenly one night, Helen's feet began to hurt. After she was rushed to the hospital, she became **paralyzed**. She was suffering from exhaustion. A virus had infected her nerves, and for a long time she was close to death. Dr. Seuss stopped working for about a year to help her recover. During that time, Helen said Dr. Seuss was really "part man, part angel."[14]

A Cool Cat

In 1955 Dr. Seuss took his readers beyond the bland and boring lessons in spelling books to a place where spelling was magic in *On Beyond Zebra*. Meanwhile, an article in

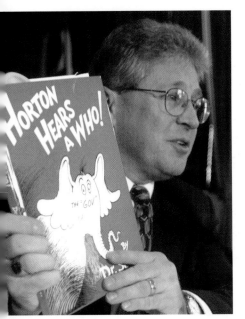

Life magazine mentioned his name as someone who could help make schoolbooks more exciting. This article inspired Dr. Seuss to write a new kind of schoolbook. To do so, he chose 225 words from a list of 400 words that first graders were supposed to learn.

Dr. Seuss tried for months to make a book with just those

Ohio senator Mike Shoemaker holds *Horton Hears a Who*.

The sneaky Grinch is pictured above.

words, but after writing several drafts, he was ready to give up. Hoping to find a new direction, he wrote *How the Grinch Stole Christmas* in a few weeks while he was still puzzling over his schoolbook project. One day he looked at the list one more time and decided that if he could find two rhyming words, he would write a book about those words.

He found "cat" and "hat," and a masterpiece was born—but not without a terrible struggle. Dr. Seuss said: "It took me a year of getting mad as blazes and throwing [the manuscript] across the room."[15] When *The Cat in the Hat* was published in 1957, it became a sensation and a wild success. The cat was a cool troublemaker, but he was never cruel, and the children loved him in school.

Beginner Books

After the success of *The Cat in the Hat*, Bennett Cerf's wife convinced Dr. Seuss to act as president of Beginner Books, his own division at Random House. Helen was made vice president, and together the Geisels searched for other authors to write books for new readers.

Meanwhile, *The Cat in the Hat* made Dr. Seuss famous. He toured the country visiting children and signing books for them. Everywhere he went he was invited to parties. The success of *The Cat in the Hat* was soon followed by *Yertle the Turtle* (about an uncaring dictator), *The Cat in the Hat Comes Back*, and the beloved Beginner Book, *One Fish Two Fish Red Fish Blue Fish*.

Dr. Seuss holds his book, *The Cat in the Hat,* a story about a lovable troublemaker.

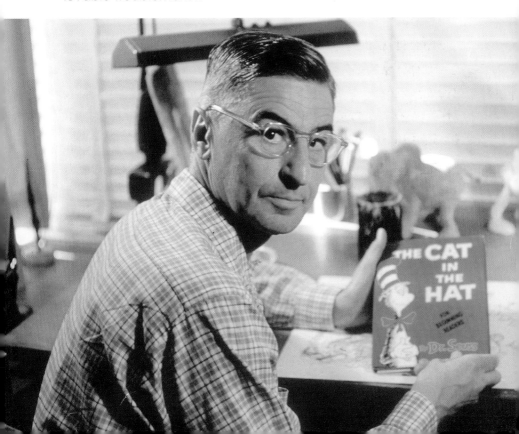

Soon Dr. Seuss had more money than he needed or wanted. He had little interest in personal wealth, but he could not refuse a good dare. One day Cerf bet him fifty dollars that he could not write a book using only fifty words. The most popular Dr. Seuss book of all, *Green Eggs and Ham*, was hatched from that bet.

When it was published with exactly fifty different words, *Green Eggs and Ham* joined five other Dr. Seuss books on the *New York Times* list of best-selling books of 1960. Some readers noticed how the story's hero Sam-I-Am drove everybody crazy, but as with the Cat in the Hat, no adults were around to make him behave.

Around this time, Dr. Seuss began to spend his days writing Beginner Books and his nights making paintings. He also worked on the animated television shows *Horton Hears a Who* and *How the Grinch Stole Christmas*.

Goodbye to Helen

Meanwhile, Helen was not well, and was becoming depressed and overwhelmed by work. She had never fully recovered from the illness in her nerves. Then one evening she took too much pain medication before bedtime. Early the next morning, on October 23, 1967, Helen Palmer Geisel died in her sleep. She had lived a very unselfish life, working tirelessly to help her husband in his work.

Ever since Helen had become paralyzed, her feet had always hurt her. In response, Dr. Seuss stayed in his studio that winter, and worked on *The Foot Book*. It was a

Dr. Seuss and his wife Helen enjoy the day outside their home in La Jolla, California in 1957.

book for very young children just learning to read, the first of the Bright and Early Books.

Using his work to help him through this difficult time, Dr. Seuss had to make a new beginning in his life—without Helen by his side.

Chapter Four

The Serious Side of Dr. Seuss

On August 5, 1968, Dr. Seuss married a family friend, Audrey Diamond Stone. In September 1969 the couple left for a seven-week trip around the world. They ended their trip in New York, where they celebrated the publication of *I Can Lick 30 Tigers Today and Other Stories*, dedicated to Audrey.

The Lorax

Back in his studio in La Jolla, Dr. Seuss watched bulldozers cut into the hills and destroy the natural habitat to build hotels, condominiums, and other big projects for tourists. He disliked the wasteful destruction of nature and wanted to write a book about the environment. But when he tried his words sounded harsh and preachy.

Dr. Seuss decided he needed a vacation, and in September 1970 the Geisels traveled to the east African country of Kenya. One afternoon, while he was reading by the hotel swimming pool, inspiration came to him. He described that moment: "About a mile away, a herd of elephants came over a hill. I don't know what happened. I

Dr. Seuss urges caring for the environment in his book *The Lorax*.

grabbed a laundry list that I had beside me and wrote the whole book in 45 minutes."[16]

His new book, *The Lorax*, offered young readers a way to fight against greed and pollution. The Lorax popped out of the stump of a chopped-down tree to speak for the trees and the animals of the forest. He said it was crazy to destroy the environment to make things that nobody needs. *The Lorax* left the message that unless someone cares enough to stop buying useless things and start restoring the environment, things will never get better.

The Butter Battle Book

Dr. Seuss was serious about making the world better. In his lifetime, he had seen terrible suffering as leaders raced to dominate the world in World Wars I and II. The United States dropped nuclear weapons on Japan in 1945 to end World War II, but the radioactive fallout continued to damage generations of innocent people there.

Despite the lessons of two world wars, the United States and the Soviet Union continued the race for world domination, developing nuclear weapons thousands of times more deadly than those dropped on Japan. Dr. Seuss could not understand how the democratic U.S. government could impose "such deadly stupidity" on people. Dr. Seuss said, "I'm not antimilitary, I'm just anticrazy."[17]

To speak out against the nuclear arms race, Dr. Seuss created *The Butter Battle Book*. The book is about two tribes who look alike, the Zooks and the Yooks, but they fight each other because the Zooks eat bread with the butter side down. The publishers argued over the cover, the title, and the story, saying it was too scary and did not have a happy ending. But in the end the book was published just as Dr. Seuss wanted it, on his eightieth birthday.

Dr. Seuss said he did not know whether it was an adult book for children or a children's book for adults. The critics could not agree on the book either. Some said the subject was too bleak and difficult for children. Others said

Dr. Seuss signs a copy of *The Butter Battle Book,* a book that had a serious point about war.

that the book would help the children to think about a question that would be very important to their future. Despite the disagreements, *The Butter Battle Book* became a best-seller all over the world.

An Obsolete Child

In 1984 Dr. Seuss won the Pulitzer Prize for giving his life to educating America's children and their parents in an enjoyable way. Dr. Seuss was amazed that such a grown-up institution would recognize him. The next year, Princeton University gave him an **honorary** doctor of fine arts degree, with these words of praise:

> He makes house calls in the land of our first dreams and fears, where naughty cats wear hats, and the menace of the Grinch is real. From Mulberry Street

to Solla Sollew he leads us through the brightly colored landscape of imagination, a place of improbable rhymes and impossible names, odd creatures and curious food. Encouraging children to read beyond zebra, to count fishes red and blue, he gives them their first mastery over the mystery of signs. He shows them the way to the adult world, as he shows adults the way to the child.[18]

Dr. Seuss still saw himself as a child. When he went to parties, he drew the Cat in the Hat on the place mats and napkins, scowling at all the fuss over fancy food. But although his mind remained fresh and young, his body was old. His illnesses, he said, included "a series of everything."[19]

Dr. Seuss spent a lot of time in hospital waiting rooms, bored and scared. He began to draw what was around him, and what he thought was going to happen to him. He made it into a book, *You're Only Old Once: A Book for **Obsolete** Children*. It was published on his eighty-second birthday on March 2, 1986. Old people and young people loved it, and it sold a million copies in the first year.

We Can Do Better

That year, Dr. Seuss had an art show, with a lifetime of his work, at the San Diego Museum of Art, which was decorated with a twenty-two-foot-tall Cat in the Hat on the roof. The show traveled around the country, and the Geisels traveled with it. Wherever Dr. Seuss went, the children showered him with love. After many years away, he went back to his hometown of Springfield, traveling in an old bus with the mayor pointing out the way the city had changed over the years.

On Mulberry Street, two hundred children, parents, and teachers welcomed him home, yelling out, "We love you, Doctor Seuss!"[20] They carried a banner that read, "AND TO THINK THAT I SAW HIM ON MUL-BERRY STREET!"[21] Small children held out their hands for him to squeeze as he walked among them. They chanted the lines from *Green Eggs and Ham*, which they all knew by heart. With tears in his eyes, he waved goodbye to the children in his hometown. He had gone so many places since he was a child on Mulberry Street.

Soon, he was back in his studio. At eighty-five years old, Dr. Seuss still worked from 10 A.M. to 6 P.M. After

In *You're Only Old Once*, Dr. Seuss (pictured) writes about growing old.

pinning up drawings that he had made over the years, he decided that hope was the theme that ran through all his work. So hope was the subject of his next book, *Oh, the Places You'll Go!* Dr. Seuss looked at the drawings, photographs, and letters from his long life. He talked to biographers, who wrote out the story of his life. When they asked if he had any message he had left unsaid, he wrote them a note that said:

A protester uses Dr. Seuss's *Lorax* to express her concern about pollution.

Any message or slogan? Whenever things go a bit sour in a job I'm doing, I always tell myself, "You can do better than this." The best slogan I can think of to leave with the kids of the U.S.A. would be: "We can . . . and we've *got* to . . . do better than this."[22]

After he wrote the note, Dr. Seuss crossed out the words "the kids of," because he thought his books about overcoming hardships and prejudice, and fighting against pollution, greed, and even nuclear war, were for young and old alike.

Dr. Seuss was coming to the end of his long life. He was tired, and he slept a lot. Once in a while, as Audrey watched over him, he would look up at her, smile like the Cat in the Hat and ask "Am I dead yet?"[23]

The beloved Dr. Seuss died in his sleep in his studio on September 24, 1991. He was eighty-seven years old.

Notes

Introduction: A Champion Among Children
1. Quoted in Theodor Seuss Geisel, *The Secret Art of Dr. Seuss.* New York: Random House, 1995, p. 8.

Chapter One: Theodor Seuss Geisel
2. Quoted in Judith Morgan and Neil Morgan, *Dr. Seuss & Mrs. Geisel: A Biography.* New York: Random House, 1995, p. 277.
3. Quoted in Morgan and Morgan, *Dr. Seuss & Mrs. Geisel,* p. 27.
4. Quoted in Morgan and Morgan, *Dr. Seuss & Mrs. Geisel,* p. 45.

Chapter Two: Dr. Seuss
5. Quoted in Thomas Fensch, *Of Sneetches and Whos and the Good Dr. Seuss: Essays on the Writings and Life of Theodor Geisel.* Jefferson, NC: McFarland, 1997, p. 94.
6. Quoted in Fensch, *Of Sneetches and Whos and the Good Dr. Seuss,* p. 95.
7. Quoted in Morgan and Morgan, *Dr. Seuss & Mrs. Geisel,* p. 80.
8. Quoted in Morgan and Morgan, *Dr. Seuss & Mrs. Geisel,* p. 81.
9. Quoted in Fensch, *Of Sneetches and Whos and the Good Dr. Seuss,* p. 74.
10. Quoted in Fensch, *Of Sneetches and Whos and the Good Dr. Seuss,* p. 139.

11. Quoted in Morgan and Morgan, *Dr. Seuss & Mrs. Geisel,* p. 101.

Chapter Three: A Few Choice Words

12. Quoted in Morgan and Morgan, *Dr. Seuss & Mrs. Geisel,* p. 135.
13. Quoted in San Diego Museum of Art, *Dr. Seuss from Then to Now: A Catalog of the Retrospective Exhibition.* New York: Random House, 1986, p. 41.
14. Quoted in Morgan and Morgan, *Dr. Seuss & Mrs. Geisel,* p. 151.
15. Quoted in Morgan and Morgan, *Dr. Seuss & Mrs. Geisel,* p. 155.

Chapter Four: The Serious Side of Dr. Seuss

16. Quoted in Fensch, *Of Sneetches and Whos and the Good Dr. Seuss,* p. 126.
17. Quoted in Morgan and Morgan, *Dr. Seuss & Mrs. Geisel,* p. 249.
18. Quoted in San Diego Museum of Art, *Dr. Seuss from Then to Now,* pp. 61, 63.
19. Quoted in Morgan and Morgan, *Dr. Seuss & Mrs. Geisel,* p. 261.
20. Quoted in Morgan and Morgan, *Dr. Seuss & Mrs. Geisel,* p. 269.
21. Quoted in Morgan and Morgan, *Dr. Seuss & Mrs. Geisel,* p. 269.
22. Quoted in Morgan and Morgan, *Dr. Seuss & Mrs. Geisel,* p. 287.
23. Quoted in Morgan and Morgan, *Dr. Seuss & Mrs. Geisel,* p. 287.

Glossary

fraternity: A social group at a college or university.

honorary: Given as an honor to show respect for good works.

insecticide: A chemical substance used to kill insects.

juvenile editor: The person in charge of publishing books for children.

manuscript: The author's copy of a book or other work, prepared for publication in print.

obsolete: No longer in use, out of style.

paralyzed: To become unable to move or act.

Pledge Week: The time when people are accepted for membership in college fraternities.

prejudice: A bad opinion formed without knowledge of the facts; a hatred or suspicion of a group based on race or religion.

publisher: One who prints, announces, and sells written material, such as books.

For Further Exploration

Books

Dr. Seuss, *The Cat in the Hat*. New York: Random House, 1957. The Cat in the Hat brightens a gloomy day.

Dr. Seuss, *Horton Hears a Who*. New York: Random House, 1954. A very large creature protects very small creatures from harm.

Dr. Seuss, *The Lorax*. New York: Random House, 1971. Describes the results of pollution and greed.

Theodor Seuss Geisel, *The Secret Art of Dr. Seuss*. New York: Random House, 1995. Paintings and sculptures Dr. Seuss made for his own private enjoyment. With an introduction by Maurice Sendak.

San Diego Museum of Art, *Dr. Seuss from Then to Now: A Catalog of the Retrospective Exhibition*. New York: Random House, 1986. Pictures of the wonderful paintings and drawings from Dr. Seuss's art show in 1986, featuring his life's work. Includes a short biography.

Maryann N. Weidt, *Oh, the Places He Went: A Story About Dr. Seuss—Theodor Seuss Geisel*. Minneapolis: Carolrhoda Books, 1994. Stories about the life and works of Dr. Seuss, with pencil illustrations by Kerry Maguire.

Jill C. Wheeler, *Dr. Seuss*. Minneapolis: Abdo and Daughters, 1992. Tells the story of the life and works of Dr. Seuss.

Website

website: www.randomhouse.com/seussville. Seussville is Dr. Seuss's playground in cyberspace; featuring games, contests, a chat with the Cat in the Hat, and information about Dr. Seuss and his works.

Index

Picture Credits

About the Authors

P. M. Boekhoff has cowritten twelve children's books and illustrated many book covers. In addition, Ms. Boekhoff creates theatrical scenics and other large paintings. In her spare time, she writes poetry and fiction, studies herbal medicine, and tends her garden.

Stuart A. Kallen is the author of more than 150 nonfiction books for children and young adults. He has written extensively about Native Americans and American history. In addition, Mr. Kallen has written award-winning children's videos and television scripts. In his spare time, Stuart A. Kallen is a singer/songwriter/guitarist in San Diego, California.